ALONG CASTLE TRAIL

BADLANDS

Formations

About 65 million years ago, the Black Hills began to form draining a shallow inland sea that had covered the region for 15 million years creating a dome nearly 8,000 feet high. As the dome rose, erosion occurred. Streams became torrents, stripping rock from the hills and carrying the sediments east to the valley where the sea had been. The streams slowed and dropped the hills' debris. Over millions of years, the valley was filled with sediments up to 1,500 feet thick. Approximately 38 million years ago, the climate of the area changed drastically. Rivers and streams made mud flats and marshes, then filled with sediments to create forests and grasslands.

VULTURE PEAK

CASTLE TRAIL

YELLOW MOUNDS

BADLANDS
National Park

BADLANDS WALL AT DUSK

CEDAR PASS OVERLOOK

DOORS AND WINDOWS TRAIL

BADLANDS
National Park

BADLANDS TWILIGHT

LAYERED BADLANDS

PEAKS, MOUNDS AND VALLEYS

BADLANDS
Formations

The erratic routes of the streams, the fluctuating rates of precipitation, the masses of volcanic ash that occasionally blew in from the west - all contributed to the patchwork layering that gives today's Badlands their distinctive banded appearance. The layers are for the most part, mudstone and siltstone, very unstable materials, so insubstantial that it is an exaggeration to call them stone. Very little sediment has been added over the last million years. Instead, the whole place is falling apart as it is being carried away by the White, Bad and the Cheyenne Rivers. It is one of the world's most rapidly dissolving landscapes. The colorful banded landscape of buttes, canyons, towers and other grotesque forms are the result of the dissection of the plain by renewed erosion.

PALMER CREEK

BEGINNING OF NOTCH TRAIL

CLIFF SHELF

DOORS AND WINDOWS TRAIL

NOTCH TRAIL

BADLANDS
Roadways

The roadways are carved around through the scenery to enhance the beauty of the Badlands. The routing took not the smoothest conventional route but the roughest and thus the most scenic. From these roadways, one can appreciate the beauty and have quick access to many trailheads providing the visitor with a first hand experience. To gaze upon these marvelous layered formations is one thing, but to actually feel the roughness of the dry, hard sediments is quiet another experience. A rainstorm changes not only the colors to vivid purples and pinks but the feel changes to a soft, sticky, slippery clay.

VAMPIRE PEAKS

ALONG BADLANDS WALL

Badlands Aerial

Ben Reifel Visitors Center
And Cedar Pass Lodge

Road Leading To Pinnacle Pass

BADLANDS TERRAIN

BADLANDS
Fossils

In terms of geological time, the sediments of Badlands National Park are relatively young, formed about 26 to 32 million years ago. This period, known as the Oligocene (al' go sen') Epoch, continues to be chronicled by the regions Paleontologists (those who study fossils). With more than 250 species of mammal fossils documented, the Badlands remains one of the world's premiere sites of Oligocene era animal studies such as the Titanothere (rhinoceros-like) and ancestral horses. With continued erosion, fossils continue to be exposed. Visitors may observe fossils right from one of the many trails in the Badlands, mindful not to touch them.

BADLANDS BONES

EXPOSED ANCIENT FOSSIL BEDS

FOSSIL TRAIL

BADLANDS
Fossils

Oredont fossil

Ancient Badlands Fossil

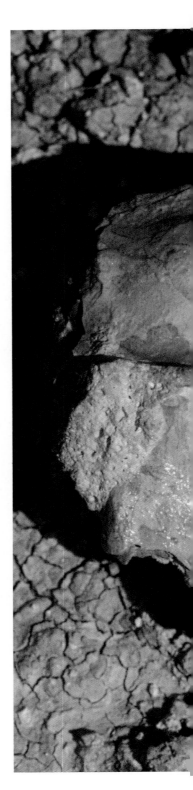

Oredont Fossil (Abundant Herding Mammal Of The Oligocene Epoch)

BADLANDS
People & Places

Visitors discover the Badlands by hiking, horseback riding and picnicking among the impressive scenery. There are numerous trails for visitors to wander on throughout Badlands National Park. Two visitors centers, the Ben Reifel Visitor Center at Cedar Pass and the White River Visitor Center located in the southerly Stronghold Unit on Hwy. 27, offer exceptional exhibits, interpretative and naturalist programs and trail maps for visitors of all ages. Both centers are staffed with knowledgeable national park rangers. Each area of the park has its own uniqueness, such as Sheep Mountain Table with its steep canyons and grassy table and Palmer Creek with its sheer peaks and heaven-bound spires. Badlands National Park has something to offer to each and every visitor.

SAGE CREEK TRAIL

SAGE CREEK RIM TRAIL

CLIFF SHELF TRAIL

BADLANDS RANCHING

BADLANDS LOOP ROAD

BADLANDS
People & Places

YELLOW MOUNDS PALESOLS

YELLOW MOUNDS PALESOLS

RED SHIRT TABLE

BADLANDS FLOWERS

BADLANDS
Wildlife

Badlands National Park is home to hundreds of prairie dogs who have carved their towns throughout the plains of the park. Jackrabbits and cottontails travel swiftly across the grasslands, where pronghorns graze. In the canyons, mule deer, coyotes and badgers may be found. In the rocky cliffs of these same canyons, white-throated swifts, swallows, rock wrens and an occasional golden eagle nest may be found. Bison and big horn sheep, which had at one time vanished from the Badlands, were reintroduced by the National Park Service and have multiplied. In the Sage Creek Basin of the Badlands, they roam and graze freely and are fully protected. The Badlands is also home to the prairie rattlesnake, bullsnakes and blotched tiger salamanders.

ROCKY MOUNTAIN BIG HORN SHEEP (SUBSPECIES OF AUDUBON, REINTRODUCED IN 1964)

BISON IN THE BADLANDS

SAGE CREEK BADLANDS WINTER

PRONGHORN ANTELOPE

BADLANDS PRAIRIE DOG

BADLANDS AT NIGHT